All That Remains

Poems by Peter Serchuk

All That Remains

Poems by Peter Serchuk

WordTech Editions

Published by WordTech Editions
P.O. Box 541106
Cincinnati, OH 45254-1106

ISBN: 9781936370771
LCCN: 2012939823

Poetry Editor: Kevin Walzer
Business Editor: Lori Jareo

Visit us on the web at www.wordtechweb.com

Cover photo: Peter Serchuk
Author photo: Gil Cope

Acknowledgements

Alehouse: "Full Moon Over Monterey Bay."

Atlanta Review: "Dallas, 1963."

Bayou: "Saturn's Chorus."

Boulevard: "The Naked Women"*, "The Old Man of the Mountain," "Beauty's Saddle," "The Last Face," " Man on Ocean Park Boulevard Talking to a Parking Meter."

Cape Rock: "Ready to Go."

Chaffin Journal: "Picasso at Ninety."

Connecticut River Review: "Fifty."

Denver Quarterly: "A School Bus Ambushed by Terrorists."

Dogwood: "The Handbook of Itches."

Fifth Wednesday Journal: "Life on Pluto," "Hiding Out in Kettle Falls."

Lullwater Review: "The End."

Mid-American Review: "My Other Life."

Margie: The American Journal of Poetry: "Abraham Lincoln as Jew." "My Allies," "The Hungry Jew," "Counting the Dead."**

Mississippi Review: "Heyday."

New Letters: "Change of Plans."

New Plains Review: "The Better Man," "The Ledge."

Nimrod: "White Rabbit."

New York Quarterly: "For the Red, White & Blue."

North American Review: "Steel Chin"***, "Surf Ballroom, 1959."

OVS: "The Girl Without a Heart."

POEM: "Memo to Summer," "Driving Lessons," "Einstein in California," "Le Bourget, 1927."

Poet Lore: "Friendly Fire."

Poetry: "Everything's for Sale."

South Carolina Review: "Trees of New England," "Stocks to Own If We Bomb Iran."

Sow's Ear Poetry Review: "The Good People."

Valparaiso Poetry Review: "Facing The Wall," "Reveille for a Winter Morning."

Worcester Review: "A Snapshot of James Wright."

*"The Naked Women" also appears in *The Best American Erotic Poems from 1800 to the Present*, edited by David Lehman (Scribner, 2(
**"Counting the Dead" also appears in *Against Agamemnon: War Poetry*, edited by James Adams (WaterWood Press, 2009).
*** "Steel Chin" also appears in *Perfect in the Art: Poems on Boxing from Homer to Ali*, edited by Robert Hedin (Southern Illinois University Press, 2003).

for Michele and Jordan, always.

Table of Contents

I

Beauty's Saddle

Beauty's in the next room
and everyone's enchanted.
She's sitting on a piano, singing
an Irish drinking song, sober
as a Monday morning.
Her silk cocktail dress is singing
too, a few inches short of breath,
while philosophers at her feet
keep filling her glass, mesmerized
by the fingers of light on her stockings.
Gentlemen, let me be clear:
she bores me to tears with her curls
and her lilts, with her hips and
her teasing. She puts me to sleep
with her spiraling promises;
like the one she's making now,
encrypted in notes you can't possibly
hear as if she were a gate swung
open wide, and me, the lone stallion
set free to roam the world.

Town Drunk

He was my wife's uncle,
married once,
diplomas from schools
most couldn't get in to.
The two of us drank ourselves
to Jupiter at my wedding, years
before he made it his profession.
People said we looked alike;
green eyes, dark hair, a look
that always seemed to be
elsewhere, as if something
invisible had entered the room.
Perhaps he saw it, that something
that told him he was not one
of the chosen, that others
would be rich or famous,
somehow noteworthy, while
his shoes would always be
brown and ordinary.
As for me, I may have seen
it too, shadowing those faces
filled with love and expectation,
a cliff too slippery to ignore,
enough to keep me sober.

Einstein in California

Though his favorite playground
sat between his ears,
he loved the fat, easy days
of a California summer.
Swinging in a hammock in Altadena,
he couldn't help but measure
the universe that had him trading
licks at the Bowl with Rodzinski
and belly laughs with Chaplin.
Flattered and feted, he calculated
the improbability of his fame;
the absurdity of the FBI in suits and ties
as they trailed him on the beach.
Later, watching the red ball of August
wade into Santa Monica Bay,
he surveyed the mass of grief
descending, his own escape,
and wondered at the fields of grace
which lace the galaxy.
Some miracles defy all understanding,
he thought. *And happiness
demands no genius at all.*

The Naked Women

Just when I thought the world
was racing to its end I see them
everywhere; ordering lattes at
Starbucks, bent over crocuses
and daffodils, waiting for buses
and taxis in earrings and heels while
morning finger-paints their backs.
On the street, joggers illuminate
the mundane. At the bank, the same
long line now seems like courtesy
thanks to the teller in Window 2.
And I marvel at the hand of justice
when a policewoman tickets
my car wearing only a pen.
What a wild world we live in,
puppets of money and fear,
as if this brief stop in Eden was
little more than a business trip.
While neighbors hoard tax cuts
and prepare for the apocalypse,
I'm comforted by the evening news;
tan lines cupping the implants of
the anchorwoman who referees
Muslims and Jews, zealots chasing
the innocent with prayer books
and guns while the meteorologist
brings a warming front to my
free and private continent.

Man on Ocean Park Boulevard Talking to a Parking Meter

Destiny, perhaps, or just good luck
took the yellow light to red and brought me
to a stop at the corner of Ocean Park and 23rd.
At first, I thought what I heard was coming
from another car—the usual hip-hop rap.
But then I saw him at the curb, talking to
the meter in front of the laundromat.
So I pulled over just to be sure he wasn't
another cell phone exhibitionist bore.
No, this was a stifled soul, an undermined heart
with something to say. It's no secret there's
enough to rant about these days and so few
ears truly listening. So I tried to listen
or at least overhear, mindful of times I've grilled
ghosts of my own with no one else there.
But his voice was garbled by traffic noise.
From his face I had to make my best guess.
My own stifled soul saw a man on a mission
for all of us, asking, *How much time is left?*

Full Moon Over Monterey Bay

No veil of mist to hide your face,
tonight I am the fog at your feet.
We know each other well, sister,
if not always by familiar light,
unmistakable by alibi.
It's been years since we've met
like this, the coils of summer past,
the great square of Pegasus
now tempting others while
we troll in the dark.
This is the cooldown,
another autumn to measure
distances, to recalibrate
the reach of hands,
to retest the polar magnets.
Yes, we will always be lovers
you and I; starved for truth,
hungry for illusion, casting
yesterday's light on the waves—
strangers when the sun comes up.

The Last Bees

Their season's over
and now they're drunk
and nasty, banging at
the screen. I can't blame
them, drunk and nasty
myself, wondering how
I wasted another summer
and dreaming of my sweet,
dead friends.

The bees buzz and bang
in their madness, dizzy
in the shrinking light,
perhaps wondering as I do
if they have loved carelessly,
if they've been blind to the hour,
if what lies beyond the screen
is silence or singing.

Pleasing the Dog

For once in this lifetime,
I know all the right spots;
just behind the ear where
her curls change color,
the down slope of her chest
just above the belly.
No fumbling with misread
cues, she throws herself on
my side of the bed, nudges
my hand to let me know it's time.
And I oblige, though not before
reminding her all pleasure is
fleeting, that even the fiercest
love has its limits. As usual,
she's bored by my protests,
certain even as I ferry her
to her bed on the floor, even
as my wife takes her place
and turns out the light,
that I am the one whose
affection will not fail;
the one true love who will
always be there with a gentle
hand, a strong arm and a
red rubber ball.

White Rabbit

The Summer of Love was over,
everywhere. It was now December
in New York, the weather and the war
bitter and getting worse. Who could
have guessed this was the calm before
the calamity, hurricanes of blood
just months away. I was only fifteen,
no LSD in my loose-leaf binder but
on the same bad trip with the rest
of America. Maybe it was a Tuesday
when I stepped off the school bus into
the four o'clock dark. Bracing myself for
the quarter-mile walk against the wind,
a flash of white caught my eye under
the corner mailbox. I walked closer,
thinking what, I don't know, maybe
someone's cat or yesterday's snow.
I bent down to look and there it was—
not snow but a snow-white rabbit.
Not Alice's or the Airplane's, this one
real and nearly frozen. I picked it up
feeling its heart race against my hand,
its two pink eyes no doubt wondering
if things had gone from bad to worse.
Do I have to tell you the odds of finding
a white rabbit, frozen or not, on a
New York City street? Or the odds of
me at fifteen, all hormones and cliché,
giving a rat's ass either way?
Jimi was asking, *Are you experienced?*
Cassius Clay was Muhammad Ali.
The Summer of Love was over,

never having made its way to Detroit,
Newark, the Sinai or Dak To.
And what had I done besides clench
my fist, cop a few feels and curse LBJ?
I was only fifteen, pathetic and small,
white and privileged as a princess phone.
The world was going to hell on roller skates.
I tucked the rabbit inside my coat
and headed home.

Keeping Kosher

My aunt wasn't much for particulars.
An apple was an apple, a bird was a bird
and a Jew was a Jew. Yes, there were
Braeburns and Galas, blue jays and robins.
But where was it written, she'd ask,
to place one above the other?
But then she fell in love with Sid,
raised an Orthodox Jew, who didn't care
much for labels but his mother did.
And when they talked of marriage
she made one thing clear: if they wanted
her blessing, theirs would be a kosher home.
So they separated the plates, banished
those for meat and dairy behind separate
gates, and the holy days would all be kept
without exception. Easy enough.
But love has its own commandments
and they both had hungers that didn't feel right
with the candles burning on Friday nights.
So they turned the basement into a haven
for overnight guests, though in 30 years
no one ever went there to find their rest.
A simple kitchen, a lovely bath, and a great
master bed. It's where they went to fry
the bacon and worship naked.

Life on Pluto

"Scientists decide Pluto is no longer a planet."
News headline August 24, 2006

With the papers signed
and the brutal game of what's
mine is mine resolved,
she reacquaints herself
with the world of men and
her maiden name.

At fifty-one, the sound
is not the same.
Nor the distance between
lost and found or
the landscape between
here and anywhere.

The landscape is unforgiving,
the distances scarred.
In search of bearings
she consults with friends
who direct her attention
to the self-help section.

Ignoring their advice,
she charts the evening sky
instead. Better to see herself
adrift in the spheres than
damaged and betrayed,
made invisible on Earth.

Bearings will come, she's
almost certain, if she can take
a cue from Pluto; calm in the dark,
never shamed by the sun and deaf
to those who ever named it
something more or less.

Saturn's Chorus

As the earth flails its arms
and swings its hips across
the solstice, Saturn sits like
a diamond pit just to the right
of the crescent moon.
And while science swears nothing
subsists on its noxious rings,
it's hard to ignore the strains
of the chorus as they float down
the galaxy into our summer night.
You've got the air,
you've got the water,
what more of the universe
could you possibly want?

The Girl Without a Heart

(AP) While she waited for a compatible transplant, 16-year-old Georgina Timmons lived without a heart for 118 days, attached to a mechanical pump. Asked what it was like, she answered, "It's like being a fake person."

She gave it away,
that rotten piece of junk,
and she never wanted it back.
She gave it away and
not to some rapper with
a tattoo on his neck
and a Rolex on his wrist.
She gave it away to Dr. Eckler
who carved it out clean as a roast,
who sliced the arteries
like wires on a bomb,
then clamped and cinched
the tubes and veins
to a pump inside her chest.
Now all she could do was
wait for her one true love,
the one destined to give
his life *and* his heart.
They hoped it might be days
(How long could she last?)
but days turned into months,
her living thread the suck
and spit of an iron fist
drumming on her ribs.
And while she waited she
drifted outside herself,

observing the girl without
a heart, a space walker
tethered to another world.
Without a human center,
what was she now,
a breathing mannequin,
a human imposter?
And what had become of
the secrets in the heart
they threw away?
Would they be waiting in
the heart that took its place?
Day after day, the metallic beat
paddled her thoughts between
here and there, vacuum and air,
between what is real and not.
Not real, she thinks, a girl
without a heart. *Not real*,
the love inside a pump.
Real, the drumming, the wires,
waiting for the dead to arrive,
to save me.

Everything's for Sale

I put the sign in the window:
Everything's For Sale.
All aisles must be cleared,
every shelf must be emptied,
room must be made at
whatever cost for whatever's
sure to arrive.

I put aside my nostalgia
for the value of things and price
accordingly; the pants I made
big promises in, the shoes
that tired too easily, the
pocket watch that couldn't
tell a day from a daydream.

Everything must go,
no matter how deep the discount.
Over here, the books yellowed
by my ignorance. In that corner,
the sheets that wrestled my
affections, the bad breath
I fed the dog.

This day belongs to bargain
hunters, to anyone who's lost
a minute's sleep guessing my
bottom line. Shortchanged
only by expectations, I lay bare
everything I paid for dearly,
everything I think I own.

At the Sanctuary for Damaged Birds

Plantation, Florida

You have to be wounded to be here.
Helpless, in fact. There's no tricking
a snowy owl, even a blind one at that.
He can smell your scourge no matter how
you dress it. His cousin, the barn owl, reckless
on one leg, has no more sympathy to give.
Every time you flinch his muscles swell,
nerves he can't remember vibrate with the love
he knows you fear.

2.
Don't pity the vulture who now answers
to "Tony." He knows you can't fly either
for all your big plans and feelings.
He made a life out of counting the dead
before a gunshot filled him with gravity.
Now, that's his heartache to live with.
What about you? he wonders.
Where will you find the steel to circle
the sky in search of purpose,
to do what must be done?
If you say, "Feed on the living,"
you'll make him laugh and wince
at the same time.

3.
The falcon's missing half a wing.
That's good enough to fly but not to hunt.
So, instead of starving in the wild he performs
his stunt with a one-eyed girl who loves

his nasty ways. If he didn't love her patch
and rats he'd slash his name across her face.
He saunters on her arm, pliant and serene,
until your pity blooms—then rockets up
to hear you scream until the chain around
his foot jerks his pride back into place.
His eyes still see a mile into the future.
His eyes are locked on every child who
calls him, "Mr. Beaker."

4.

To no one's great surprise, an eagle steals the show.
Regal in his silence, he unfurls his wings
a full eight feet to let us know his splendor.
Impressed, we wonder what could *his* affliction be?
We search for scars and deformities.
He's perfect, the girl tells us, *every inch of him.*
And so we learn not all magnificence comes naturally.
It seems eagles must learn how to be their own master.
For all his strut and royal crown, this one's an imposter;
can't hunt, can't fly, not even mate. "Adopted" as a chick,
he couldn't survive a sparrow's life alone.
Yet he plays the part so well, as if there's some mistake,
plays the part so well, we're mesmerized by his human face.
Beautiful and broken, perfect and yet not,
loved passionately by a one-eyed girl for all
he was and will never be again.

II

All-Stars

My heart belongs to you, Mickey Mantle,
flask in your locker, knees of knotted pine,
launching rockets from either side,
sweating yourself sober in center field,
eyes still crossed from last night's bender.
And you, Wilt Chamberlain, Armageddon
descending to the net, rejecting the dreams
of tiny white men, crashing backboards
with your muscle and headboards with your sex
so all could love and despise the sheer size of you.
And you, Muhammad Ali, hands too fast
for physics, face too pretty for cuts and scars,
shuffling your way to the top of the world for
a round with God, then falling, falling, falling...
a beautiful ruin but still on your feet.

Trees of New England

"That's the problem writing about New England...all the trees knew Robert Frost personally."

Charles Simic

It's true, they all knew him,
but few really liked him.
He stole secrets never meant
to be repeated and sold them
to tabloids crazy for rhymes.
They saw how he brooded in public
and screamed in whispers, all
the while free to love and bleed.

Jealous, they embraced his
contradiction, pitied his smallness
and his season, the scattered
seeds he foraged on the ground.
They knew him at his root,
half giant, half dwarf; no limb
quite tall enough for the shelf
of mysterious things.

Ready to Go

It's 10:00 AM, two days before Christmas
and my father's ready to go. A week after
doctors drilled steel screws in his back
he's pain-free for the first time all year.
And what a year it's been: falling off
a toilet, tripping in the street, his foot
sliced by a bedpost then suddenly,
gangrene. Without a by-pass in his calf,
the leg's lost below the knee.
Like always, he's toughed it out, as if
three heart attacks, two angioplasties
and a pacemaker weren't enough to
make him think, *Enough already.*
But there he stands, list in hand, ready
to brave the snow. *Let's go,* he calls to
my sister, impatient as ever, coupons
in his pocket ready to buy back his life.
Kleenex, artichokes, olive oil and string beans.
At eighty, my father knows the price of
things, the treasure of work, having some
place to be, and what a worthless friend
pride is when others feed and bathe you.
My sister is his angel, blind as a mother,
better than a son, all light, no favors.
She's nursed him for months, racing to
doctors, dressing his nerves and stitches.
Now he watches as she races to find her coat
and keys, knowing the endless lines she'll
stand in for him, knowing only love buys
what can't be repaid. *Let's go,* he says
again when the ice pick hits his chest.

Like a boxer, he stumbles back a step
then crumbles to the floor. My sister's
on him in a breath, begging him to breathe.
He thinks he hears her scream as he reaches
for the door. Desperate to hold him back,
she dials the paramedics but it's his voice
that answers somewhere down the line.
Out of time, with no more heart to give,
Don't do it, he says. *Don't do it.*

My Father's Friend Henry

Henry was handsome, tanned
and newly rich. He liked fine cigars
and the shine of other men's wives.
While the men tended to their money
Henry lent a gardener's hand
to the slender reeds they'd married.
Henry was sunshine in their bartered lives
but Henry didn't come from money.
He'd stumbled into its pocket.
And when he did he weeded out
the middle-class wife, the sometimes-sex
and split-level house he called his life.
He wanted to live like Sinatra.
He wanted the Cadillac, the pinky ring,
nightclubs where you slipped the maître d'
a fifty and he memorized your face.
But Henry wasn't Sinatra.
Seasons changed. The money withered.
Desperate to keep his tan, he planted
himself in Vegas trying to win it back.
He bet the pinky ring. He bet the Cadillac.
When the loan sharks took everything
but his life, the garden emptied,
the wives went back to their husbands
as if the weather had never changed.
My father went to see him after a stroke
left him broke and broken, not a soul
left to impress. He cried and looked away
when my father took his hand.
Henry, my father said,
there's no shame between friends.

A Snapshot of James Wright

I met him once in class,
his pants painted with ashes,
his throat still flush with smoke and song
for his Ohio and his Annie.
He wasn't what I had in mind
as poets go, not a trace of rogue
or rebel. Bookish, even professorial.
I'd imagined bass not treble.
Hard to see this imposter slicing
northern pike or on the skids in Minneapolis.
He said Horace was his Shakespeare;
Verona would always be his capital.
So I decided to be a pest and asked
about the executed man, George Doty.
When we turn killers into victims
who bears the moral responsibility?
It seemed every pencil dropped
at my stupidity or my nerve.
Doesn't a man put to death for murder
merely get what he deserves?
Any scale could have weighed the silence.
You'd hear more breathing in a tomb.
I loved the man who wrote that poem
but couldn't see him in the room.
Then the "professor" removed his glasses
so we were both now slightly blurred.
That's for a better poet, James Wright said,
I just hope I don't get what I deserve.

Abraham Lincoln as Jew

Suddenly, it all makes sense;
the beard, the hat, the face pocked
with worry. In another time and place
he might have butchered chickens or
dickered linens in the market.
Naturally, Harvard wouldn't have him.
A thousand miles away, they could
smell the onions on his breath.
Better one less Jewish lawyer hell-
bent on mankind or its money.
Abe didn't care. His world was mapped
by rain and sun, drought and mites,
prayers cut for every season.
In New Salem people didn't see much
difference between a farmer and a Jew.
How could anyone know he was already
hearing voices, already whispering
to the cotton burning in the field?
He leveled his soul to the state line.
Never color blind, he was afraid of God.
And so he prayed and prayed hard.
Put on *tefillin* every morning and a *tzitzit*
underneath his shirt each day.
On the Springfield Sprint to Washington
he joked in Yiddish with the porter.
It was a laugh too small for history.
New orders were on their way.
Before Spring could wash the White House
door, fires scorched his every dream
while a shofar bleated reveille.
Joseph himself came to unmask the blaze;
another sacrifice of flesh and blood.

One child already buried, Abe feared
to ask which one. Naive for all his faith,
he puzzled at the prophet's words.

All of them.

Picasso at Ninety

Picasso at ninety,
steady with his hands,
railed at the softness in his pants.
For the first time in his life
he was five foot four and shrinking,
disappearing into the visible world
he had always painted his way out of.
So what if he'd lived a dream
of dreams, unblinded worlds,
a bull with paint and pussy?
So what if women bent this way
and that to be held by his eye.
Without the hardness what was he
now if not flaccid, if not dying—
a god disappearing inch by inch.

Hot Rod

It's alright if you can't remember him.
After ten years in the minors almost nobody did
except Casey, who laughed when he thought about
the crazy kid who went crashing into walls
after balls that were half-way to heaven.
It was '61 when they cooked-up the Mets from
the leftovers of the league—Thornberry, Woodling,
Chacon and Bouchee, soon-to-be retirees
like Hodges and Ashburn and the one-and-only
Rod Kanehl who finally got his shot at the Show.
When you've lived in the minors for a decade
you know what it means to take the field
at the Polo Grounds, to chew the same grass
as Stanky, Irvin, Maglie and Mays, step into
the same box as Bobby Thomson when
he sent all of Brooklyn packing to Crete.
Wherever he walked Rod dug in his cleats,
hoping an ounce of the magic would stick.
But an ounce of magic wouldn't do the trick
against Koufax, Spahn or Marichal or a rocket
off the bat of Aaron or Clemente.
The fans loved him but the hand of God
was elsewhere. Fifty errors in three years,
an easy out most days except July '62,
when he took Sadecki uptown and put the Mets'
first grand slam into the record book.
That was a swing to remember, the pain of
ten seasons eclipsed, yet by '64 he was finished,
shipped down to Triple A and out of the game.
When Casey died in '75, it was an All-Star line-up
at Forest Lawn; Whitey, Billy, Scooter and Mickey
and one utility player tucked off to the side.

Hot Rod Kanehl, his restaurant closed for
the morning, palmed the baseball in his pocket,
the one-and-only Amazing Met to say goodbye.

Dallas, 1963

For a moment we thought
we were all handsome and rich,
that it was our old man who'd schemed
his way into millions, who taught us
the ropes and strings to pull in any fish.
We weren't deluded just bored,
and we loved our borrowed life;
hands unspoiled by work,
the haircut and witty quips,
touch football on the great lawn
and just a whiff of sex.
Besides, a new decade was banging
its elbows on the door, insisting
we pack up yesterday's fears.
We hadn't blown ourselves up after all
and here we were, a year later,
talking about a "free" world
and dancing toward the moon.
Somehow it was all going to be just fine:
Cuba, Oxford, and Khrushchev.
Suddenly the future was something
worth waiting for. And we were waiting,
like roses cocked to the sun, waiting
with our children and our flags
and our Dr. Pepper, waiting for our
chariot to turn the corner of
Houston and Elm.

The Last Face

Unconscious for a week
and melting down, it's hard
to know what anyone might see.
But since it was my mother
sleeping on the fence, I knew it
wasn't Jesus standing in the light
or even Captain Roussand,
her one true love, who wouldn't
leave his Catholic wife.
I held her hand, now lighter than
a glove, and reminded her
the air was clear above her bed.
And in the moment just before
her hand dropped down, I guessed
it was her mother's face she found.
60 years ago, their roles had been
reversed; my mother's teenage face
a sobbing moon above the bed.
For 60 years she memorized her life
within those satin eyes and where
she landed when they closed,
loveless in a world of men.

Heyday

for my father

We wore fedora hats
and ate nickel sandwiches,
played johnny-on-the-pony
and pitched copper pennies.
We worked all day, dreamed
of marrying saints and after
hours ran straight up to Harlem.

It was a good time to be a man,
a good time to know your way
around the block and a dollar.
Once you knew who lived where
and why you had friends
for life and rules to live by.
Bright Eyes owned the bar on
President Street. He only let his
sister in after hours. Even with a mop
in her hands she smelled like chocolate
and flowers and made you dream
about her dress on a hanger.

The war was still a world away
and Brooklyn still a world of its own.
Friday nights we'd take the train to
Ebbets Field or maybe split a cab
to Coney Island. From the top of
the Steeplechase you could fly across
Queens, or scratch your back on
the Empire State Building.

Only the Rockefellers and Vanderbilts
were rich. The rest of us shuffled
ends and means, drove our trucks,
stitched our seams and gave our ears
and our pay to Mr. Roosevelt's plans.
"I like his voice," Bright Eyes' sister
said, wiping her hands on the back
of her jeans. Not much for politics,
I stared anyway. The right girl could
change your mind about anything.

The Hungry Jew

Yankee Stadium, 1965

Yom Kippur is how you separate
the Jews from the jews.
Not Chanukah or Purim with their latkes
and laughter, not Shavuot or Tu B'Shevat...
God himself can't remember the months.
And Rosh Hashanah, holy as it is,
trumpets one more circle, a clean step forward,
as unJewish an idea as happiness itself.

But Yom Kippur, when we feast
on the same dust left to Moses above Canaan,
on the same dust that bore witness to
Hank Greenberg's giant shoes, that's when
we tell Him that we, the chosen ones, are here
to earn His blessings, to beg His forgiveness
no matter whose game or rules.
That's why today, World Series be damned,
that's handsome Don Drysdale on the mound
and not the hungry Jew, Sandy Koufax.

Le Bourget, 1927

We were merry from the wine
and the perfumed skirts.
We were drunk on the marriage
of man and machine, drunk enough
to bring our wives and our mistresses.
Farmers brought their children,
children brought their dogs and pigs.
Lindbergh est arrivé!
Lindbergh est arrivé!
People waved whatever was in
their hands—flags, scarves, cheese
and bread, waved goodbye
to yesterday and sipped
the Beaujolais Nouveau.
We were new ourselves and lighter
than air, reinventing the world as we
stood in the fog of the future.
But what madness must have
raced through his mind as he
descended into our mayhem?
What vision of the life ahead as we
raced across the field to raise him
up to immortality and suffering,
his wheels never again to touch
the ground so lightly.

Dropping Dead

When they called to say
you'd dropped dead on the back nine,
I forgot to ask your score.
Or whether the greens were fast
or slow, if your slice had kept you
in the sand or whether your putting
was worth a damn.

The truth is I forgot to ask
about you. I asked about your wife
and son, who else knew;
about your sister whose wailing
I could already hear having buried
your parents just last year.

Or maybe I just wasn't surprised
and guessed that neither were you.
With your father's rusted, hand-me-down
heart they said you wouldn't make it
past heart attack two. So you laughed
and lived and drank and smoked,
knowing not even saints steal
the devil's joke.

Still, I wish I'd been there
keeping score, to cough each time
you tried to swing, to hiss
each time you found the woods
and say some small, unspoken thing
about the days you'd leave behind,
the missing lines inside your fist.

Of course we'd never say such words.
The talk would have been of songs
and beer. A six-pack each through
fourteen holes, sweat dripping through
old football shirts, the books we'd
never give away, the girls who
let us sail their skirts.

Still, I wish I'd been there to play
fifteen, watch you nail that putt
from twenty feet. You gave
your white boy Southern yelp,
no one guessed the word was *help*,
just a birdie for ole General Lee.

But in my dream I add an extra
beat, I slow the scene a frame
or two. You sink the putt and get
your yelp, you ask the score
and I say, *Fuck you.*

Then we're back in sync
as your eyes roll up but I'm off the cart
before you drop; and I catch you
before you hit the past,
before the scene goes dark
I get to say, *Nice shot.*

Steel Chin

George Chuvalo was a punching bag,
face full of blood, spitting out teeth.
A tough kid scraped off the Toronto streets,
he sparred with the wind and the cops and the thugs.
He ate in the church with the beggars and nuns
and learned crowds never stay once a man hits the ground.
No matter the punch, no matter the round,
George Chuvalo never went down.
The best fighters in the world reconfigured his face.
Hockey's for punks, he liked to say.

Elegy for a New Jersey Poet

You too would have loved him, Dr. Williams.
Like you, he saw everything too small for the ambitious eye
and marveled at its place; slugs climbing out to taste
the rain, caterpillars hiking the leaf of uncertain change,
ants busy with the labor of the world.
While others honed their heartache for the moon,
he tuned his ear to a cricket's bow.

Any poet can fall in love with heaven.
This one loved New Jersey;
not Short Hills, Morristown or Englewood Cliffs—
but Paramus, Brunswick and Orange,
the anonymous life where nobody cares who owns
Manhattan or who sits in what chair in Princeton.
How better to learn of darkness and light
than snowfall on the Jersey Turnpike?

He didn't get the chance to be old and wise, Dr. Williams.
He had to memorize what he loved in half the time,
to have his say in half as many words.
Imagine the rest of us trying to live like that.
Imagine us holding our tongues, staring off into
the New Jersey night where our children live on
without us, content to be famous with those we love.

Surf Ballroom, 1959

We nearly froze to death outside
the Surf but Donna would have died
a thousand times before missing
Ritchie Valens. I knew, for sure, that
she loved Dion and The Belmonts more
but Ritchie won her heart when he
put her name top of the charts.

Still, we were teenagers in love
though I wasn't big on the sweet stuff
or hot on the bop of The Big Bopper.
It was Buddy I wanted to see, hiccups
and all, a curiosity parked behind those
windshield teeth and bug-eyed glasses.

No, Buddy didn't look like Elvis
or Jerry Lee. He'd never be anyone's
check-out line fantasy but he didn't care.
He wasn't singing for the swoons.
He wasn't singing to your girl in her room
like some vinyl gigolo. Buddy was singing
for his girl and he sang it like a man.

He opened with *Oh Boy!*, *Maybe Baby*,
and *Everyday*. Then *Raining in My Heart*,
and *That'll Be the Day*.
The hall was jumpin', that's for sure,
but Buddy didn't play it cool;
not even with a tease like *Peggy Sue*.

It was just rage and want and hurt
and thrill. I couldn't play six notes but

I felt the chords and when he growled
It Doesn't Matter Anymore, it shook me up.
I wondered if the other boys on their way
to men felt the same wild punch
that I felt then.

I was dazed and drained when the lights
came up. People whooped and screamed
at that empty stage. Not a soul
had budged when he came back out
and sang, *Rave On!* We bent the floor
when he waved goodnight and said, "So long."

The streets were slick so I took it slow.
Donna gushed the whole way home
though I barely said a word.
Outside her door we feigned romance
but once I heard the deadbolt click
I made my way back to the Surf
and wiped away that teenage kiss.

The cars were gone, the Surf pitch black,
though around the back stood one last bus.
I asked if Buddy was still in town,
I had the wheels to track him down
but the driver said I was out of luck.
He laughed out loud and pointed up.

So I sat until he pulled away, heard him
grind those gears to the Interstate.
I could picture Buddy, guitar and beer,

already flying high to tomorrow's show.
With the windows down and the heater up
I punched the dial and scanned the clouds
but it was too late now for rock & roll.

The Old Man of the Mountain

May 3, 2003 (AP): The Old Man of the Mountain, the enduring
symbol of the State of New Hampshire, is no more. Some time
between Friday evening and Saturday morning, the stone profile
that draws hundreds of thousands of visitors to Franconia Notch
State Park each year collapsed.

Once upon a time,
back five thousand years,
he perched his chin off Cannon Mountain
and dared the weather make him old.
He was young and indestructible as
young is, a twin of God and time,
and nothing ahead and nothing behind
advised he'd ever wear out his welcome.

Once upon a time,
he was five granite ledges climbing clouds,
gouged by an ice sheet melting and slipping,
cutting and creeping into Franconia Notch.
Then suddenly we appeared in the mud bath
below with our tepees, our bibles, our postcards
and Winnebagos, thinking we stood in the gaze
of God's imagination.

He was five granite ledges
out heaven's door, but sooner or later
men grow weary or bored from the weight
of their own myths. Sooner or later
every man feels gravity lasso his knees

and tug at the view of all he's loved,
the world he once knew,
once upon a time.

He was five granite ledges
but nothing more, and sooner or later
everything falls despite the cables
and bolts, the pulleys and prayers,
until only memories hold them up.
Today I buried my father of 51 years
then drove half a day up old 93,
to see what was left of eternity.

III.

Change of Plans

There's been a slight change in plans,
We won't be staying after all.
And such a beautiful place in its way—
Wherever you look someone's gasping for hope
Or racing for a pint of blood.
We had grander plans but soft currency.
Now it's back to the things we know;
Feeding the dog his cat, the cat his mouse,
And the mouse his big dream of cheese.

2.
If you haven't heard, we're rich.
We've patented the chatter of teeth.
Call it my musical ear, but I hear
A chorus of chewing.
Now, to swallow or spit is the question.
There's good news for the dead,
They'll never go hungry
And never have to floss.

3.
Mum is the word from our Maker.
No guarantee mail will be forwarded.
Our prayers are the ether that put him
To sleep, fogged the mirror above our bed.
Some say he'll be back to tidy up,
The rest say he's already been.
Any damn fool can see our pickle,
We're a world that's sweet on tough guys.
A world confused by wise men,
Addicted to bullets and french fries.

Tending to the Homeless in Santa Monica

My wife has a heart of gold
although not always for me,
so when we left the Pizza Palace
with half a pie still warm in the box
she had to stop when the homeless
man called from the floor of a storefront.
Unshaven, filthy, yet with a face
that cried victim of circumstance,
he said he was hungry. Could we spare
some change? Aware of God's grace
and how easily fates change with just
a few breaks, I reached into my pocket
for the world's compassion.
Here, take this, my wife said,
handing over the box before
I could offer a bill. How crass of me,
I thought, to find a soul in need
and think only of currency.
He took the box with the most
grateful of eyes, peeked inside
and handed it back. My wife turned
to me, her face in a quandary.
Nice thought, he said,
but I don't do dairy.

Hiding Out in Kettle Falls

The police won't find him here.
He's carved himself into the mountain,
a face not even the weather can recognize.
All winter his footprints die in circles.
When he drives past, neighbors
wave to his ghost.

2.
In August, he comes down to buy
our peaches, not the orbs that drench
your shirt but culls you jar, three pounds
for a dollar. We talk about the orchard
and the river, what takes root
and what glides by.

3.
Rumors are ripe about his past.
Some say he's done terrible things,
others worry what he might do again.
Hypnotized by fear, most are desperate
to be his friend, to pardon the misfit
of their curiosity.

4.
The alibis are air-tight, his and ours.
Nobody stands before a court of men
without his real life well-hidden.
From our ladders high in the trees,
we watch his tires lift a curtain of dust
and disappear into summer.

Driving Lessons

In fog like this, maps don't work.
It's a bad stretch from here to the river,
no shoulders, all guesswork, a nervous foot
on the pedal, signs that can't be read
no matter how hard you pray.
Whenever you see a flash of light
it's either God or an eighteen-wheeler.
To fend off panic, I feign control;
search mirrors for clues, scan
the dial for loyal frequencies.
The rock & rollers want me stripped
of all caution, my middle finger stiff
in the face of uncertainty; and just
when I think I can lift those dice and roll them,
some country bubba croons about
all I've got to lose.

I wasn't prepared for this weather,
wasn't prepared to be taking this curve
blind, a wallet fat with obligations,
hands slippery from compromise
and accommodation. By now
I expected to be cruising the Interstate,
every lane fast and familiar.
I take deep breaths, try to picture
the lines I drew for myself back
when the weather was clear.
Wasn't this the road I insisted on driving,
the topography I so carefully rendered?
Or did I nod off and drift to the right,
the darling of slow-moving traffic?

Leaning back in my seat, I curse the sleep
in my eyes and flash my brights on the world.
I unfasten my belt, let go of the wheel,
become the fool this fog wants to love.

Facing the Wall

There was no good reason,
he told himself over and over.
He repeated this again and again
to his wife and daughter,
to mourners at the church,
to the mineshaft in the mirror.
There was no good reason,
he reminded neighbors in
the kitchen, faces at the office,
the phone that froze the clock.
All eyes were on him to explain,
to assign logic to the wall,
to the hand that lost its grip,
to the fall that should have gouged
a knee or beat an elbow black
and blue but not the universe.
There was no good reason,
he told the wall itself, night after
night, the wall with no sight,
no saints, no arms to catch
what falls, the one oblivious to
circumstance and consequence,
oblivious to his beautiful boy,
the wall strangers would point
to for years to come as *that* wall
where *it* happened, the one
that divided his days into past
and present, darkness and light,
the one he too could only face
but not climb over.

A Photograph of My Mother at 36

She's beautiful and telling you
she's everything she hoped to be;
the favored child, an unmistakable
success, footsteps strangers follow
and a woman who married well despite
the Russian name. Staring into her face,
I'm inclined to believe her now. After all,
she was some of that, like a hyacinth
is some of Spring, like a kiss from
any mouth is some of love.
If only she could have lived inside
this frame the way we all want to live
inside our secret life and dreams.
She tried to believe in happiness
but other faces soiled the view;
a husband and life she couldn't love,
the mother who died too young and
strip-mined her heart. To fill the hole,
she drilled other holes, became the mistress
of other sorrows. Imagine being so right
for this world, wounded and selfish,
only to have the selfish world turn away.
Baffled, she pleaded with God but he
was just another man short on answers.
Resigned, she struck an uneasy truce
with a smaller world and set her own sights
on an early death—never guessing
she'd find peace here, on a bookshelf,
her life nearly picture perfect.

The End

It took a week,
six days longer than anyone's guess.
Lungs glued to each breath
like sucking golf balls through a straw,
she knew the devil had her soul
but he wasn't getting it for free.
He wasn't getting anything without
a screaming kick in the balls.
My mother always played for keeps,
nothing easy.

So we watched the sun float
up and down, drank scotch and beer;
told stories she would have liked
to hear if she wasn't all teeth and bones.
We tried not to be frightened by fate.
The doctor called with his regrets,
comfortable, at last, with his diagnosis.
Hold her hand, tell her it's alright to let go.
You got the wrong lady, mister.
Here's her dying words:
After you.

Fifty

At fifty, one thinks...
if I am not the blazing sun
rousing the grain to hallelujah,
if I am not the leaf blown free around
the world, if I am not the string on
whose throat the music plays
then who am I?

At fifty, one thinks...
maybe I am not the wild heart,
maybe not the pearl in ice,
maybe not quite over average
but only flat light on the river,
at best a passing cloud,
an everyday promise.

Fifty is when you wake, suddenly
short of breath and regrade
the ladder of expectations;
when you have a heart to heart
with your bladder and bowels,
with your heart and your sex,
fearful of surprises.

Fifty is when surprises
howl and contradictions rule.
Fifty is when you confess that
nobody had the right hunch
about you, uncertain now
if the bullets dodged didn't
take out better men.

The Ledge

Shall we be dazzled or afflicted?
she asked, the eye of the moon
half-shut, a new century of men
already defending their right to die.
She was twenty years younger
and I was out on that ledge where
the ground is no longer visible
and men lose their fear of heights.
But I knew the ground, had taught
myself to walk straight-faced on
its nails once God stopped listening.
The ground was no place to live
or love, and everything above
now a dangerous illusion.
I had my own illusions, no need
of the ventriloquists insisting we
march the long road to paradise.
Dazzled or afflicted? I kissed her
as if she were my only hope,
my only way of saying, *Both.*

The Philanthropist

I gave a hundred to St. Jude's
and a hundred to the blind.
A hundred to fight the floods
and a hundred to fight the fires.
I gave one-fifty to the Red Cross
though I couldn't spare the blood.
The homeless got a hundred
because I love my king-size bed.
Two hundred to the hospice
that walked my mother to the door.
For the food bank, thirty cans
and a check for thirty more.
Fifty to Meals on Wheels.
Fifty for Jerry's kids.
Twenty to the Girl Scouts for
the mints I'll never eat.
The church, three Christmas turkeys
to ignore my empty seat.
I gave fifty to the Rotary just to
get them off my back.
And a hundred to Goodwill plus
a rack of tired clothes.
The opera got a hundred because
Violetta's still my girl.
One-fifty to save Darfur.
Fifty to save the whales.
Two hundred went to AIDS research
because it ate a friend alive.
I gave fifty to the Policemen's Fund
for the sticker on my car.

Two hundred for the veterans
for the tours I never served.
The politicians nothing for
the nothing they deserve.

Michigan Winter Landscape, Painter Unknown

He must have hated this ground
or maybe loved what he feared.
Every brush stroke seems to whisper,
Please, don't bury me here.

Everything's grey, even the wind.
A sky birds never cross. Everywhere
snow weighs on the ground, intent
on locking everything down.

At the edge, lower right, the remains
of a fence and a hint of animal tracks—
as if they'd come to the edge of the world
and had the good sense to double back.

Memo to Summer

Like you, I promise nothing.
To a house blistered by ice I bring
a season of heat, throw some light
into corners left blind and forgotten.
Like you, my days are measured,
my heart slanted to angles
polished by the clock.

People bruise so quickly in the cold,
expectations plunge when morning
knocks still dressed in black.
Then you and I come back,
another season pruned, to plant
whatever sings and sighs under
the cotton moon.

The Truth About Clouds

Some days, they spread out like milk
or stack themselves like Buddhas.
Moody and unreliable, that's their charm.
Here for lunch and then they're gone.

The principles of weather bore them.
They rant and roar when they damn well please.
They never steal a glance at passing planes
or peek below their knees.

They leave longing to the moon, worship to
the sun. As hitchhikers, they're famously free.
Stick with stars to wish for a life less sad
and planets for a place to plant your flag.

The Better Man

I try to picture myself as
the better man, one whose
heart never picks yesterday's
pocket, whose eyes are clear
enough to enter a room without
looking for a back door.
As the better man, I end
my negotiations with God
over doubt and grace.
The better man reminds me
to be grateful for what
others can't give, for stars
too deep in their own dark
to point to a familiar port.
We stare each other down
in the hallway mirror hearing
old desires rattle their spoons,
wondering who'll blink first,
each thinking the other
is the mirage.

My Other Life

He owns a smoke shop, the bastard.
He reads books that take months to get through.
He says, *Go ahead, live a little*, to strangers
when they sniff an expensive cigar.
This is the man who lives my other life.
A master of smoke and other disguises.

2.
A miserable failure, he covets nothing
I envy: not the women or the money,
not the hot thigh of success.
He admires my persistence, the leather of my skin.
He admires my insistence on answers.
A man with a future, he says with a smile.

3.
I ask if I can help, mix the burleys and Virginias,
sort the meerschaums and the briars.
I ask if I can sleep with his wife,
steal the love of his children,
drink the last of his brandy.
He laughs as if I'd made a joke.
He hands me the keys to his empty house.

The Handbook of Itches

1. The Nuisance
Soothe it while it's small,
as if it were a child pouting
for attention. Ignored it might
return to silence only to
plan a lifetime of revenge.
Why take chances?
Let some other be the one
who teaches disappointment.
Scratch it now while the need
is still a question, as if it were
a spaniel waiting at the door:
something you give a minute's
love for a lifetime of devotion.

2. The Gypsy
A restless itch is trying to
teach you something of desire.
It's never in the same place twice.
When you think you have it cornered
on a toe, it lights a match behind
your knee or marches ant-like
across your shoulder.
The remedy? Don't try to sleep.
This is a call to wakefulness.
Time to bring up the lights
and clean out the drawers.
Time to unpack the apologies
and regrets and let whatever
breathes unfold.

3. The Insatiable
There is evil in all of us
and we must learn to dig it out.
The itch runs deep and masks
its face beneath a sheet of pleasure.
The more we scratch, the more
it purrs. The more it purrs,
the more we scratch and bleed.
True pleasure is a measured feast
while evil lives to gorge.
To root it out, it must be starved.
It must be starved but not ignored.

4. The Blessing
It's always in a place we can't
quite reach, despite our best
contortions. Forget the sticks
and forks, the trees and doorposts.
Forget the awareness peddlers
and do-it-yourselfers.
This is the light in Plato's cave,
the elastic thread between wave
and shore, every God in heaven
distilled down to his best day.
How we lay our hands on the world
is all we can say of our souls.
It's there, right there, no, a little
to the left, now up, just a hair...
Tell me, sister, did I get it?

IV

My Allies

*Today everybody is with Hamas because Hamas won the battle. If Fatah
had won the battle they'd be with Fatah. We are a hungry people, we are with
whoever gives us a bag of flour and a food coupon. Me, I'm with God and a
bag of flour.*
                    Yousef, age 30. Gaza, 2007

Today, Yousef, I am not with Hamas.
Nor with Fatah, Hezbollah, Taliban or Al Qaeda.
Don't mistake me for a man of conscience
for I have many bags of flour and a family
that could stand to lose a little weight.
Still, believe me if you can when I say I'm not with
the Syrians, the Saudis, the Persians or Israelis.
By now, it's no secret. So little of what I try
to say rings true. But if God is with the living,
Yousef, then I'm with him and with you.

Reveille for a Winter Morning

Lovers in their bed breathe easy.
Inmates in their cells care less.
The man with a job wakes to his weight
while the man without wakes to his wall.

It's a good day to be a farmer,
the sky clear of omens and the soil already turned.
Yesterday's money means nothing now.
Winds graze the field where fruit once fell.

The Jesus That I Love

Back for a refresher
course, he crosses the border
face-down in a van,

walks past a fruit stand
just as it blows and
waits in a desert,

as black as it's white,
blooming with bones.
This time, he's not so

happy to be the Christ
and not so happy to be
a man or anyone

descended from Abraham.
Making the rounds
from Belgrade to Beirut,

Tel Aviv to Tehran,
Pyongyang, Khartoum,
Washington and Lahore,

he remembers again
the suffering forsaken,
the cross that saved him

from the world and
the centuries he swore
never to return.

This time around,
he knows nothing can
be left to miracles

or preaching, nothing
can be left floating
in the air. *This time,*

he says, *I will be light
everlasting. This time,
I'm not going anywhere.*

The Sick Minister

At 72, he's not well.
His heart and his liver have both
complained. His skin looks like an old rug
that's seen too many wine spills
and his eyebrows have abandoned
all latitude in search of the host
whose signal he's lost.

It's been a rough decade
for believers, especially those
whose God doesn't hunt infidels
or homosexuals. After 40 years
of preaching doubt as a ladder,
he stands in the pulpit with vertigo,
hears creaking rungs below.

Surely it's time, he thinks.
Hasn't the scalding tide already
breached the highest wall?
Laying the body of Christ upon
the tongue of the congregation,
his ears reach for the horns of Jericho,
impatient for the incarnate to appear.

Two nights later and half a bottle
closer to the heel of his thirst,
he invokes the savior to empty
his glass of all knowledge
and urge, to lay him down blind
under that poisonous tree,
out of the devil's reach.

Instead, the wine and weariness
embrace in his eyes and what he
sees is a view from a different cross.
No one below to weep for his soul
he shouts, *I am the free man
created in haste, the son hurled
into the void.*

Stocks to Own If We Bomb Iran

Go long on alternative energy,
specifically kindling and matches.
Go short on fruit and chocolate
for nothing will taste sweet.
Diamonds are a buy, as millions
search for light but gold's
just a hold unless it tassels
an ear of corn. Times like these
scream with opportunity but
it takes a contrarian to bank
the last laugh. My best tip?
Invest in the inevitable:
shovels, urns and caskets.
Follow the charts to the jackpot
underground. Sell retail, travel,
and recreation. Sell any real estate
not attached to heaven.
Currencies? Maybe,
but only if they're edible.
Futures? Seriously?
Haven't you been listening?

For the Red, White & Blue

"You Americans are all alike—a mile wide and an inch deep."
          remark by an Englishman at a party

Our brains are thin as wafers,
our souls stack in the sink,
and our compassion—one vast
pizza minus the pepperoni.
It's a sad state of affairs from
Napa to Nantucket: an entire
nation descended not from
Chaucer and Shakespeare
like yourself, but from frisbees
and flounder. Armies of gentlemen
much like you have gone mad
drilling for substance, wildcatting
for conscience only to hit
pop tarts and bowling shoes.
And isn't it just like us, old chap,
instead of being shamed and
ready to have our knickers
knocked, we're laughing our
plaid heads off like some wag
out of Charlie Dickens;
frolicking in the shallow end
of existence, spread thin as pie
crust from Miami to Monterey.
You've got us bloody pegged,
old man, knee-high to pig's feet,
no Queen, no Bloomsbury,
no clotted cream and jam,
traitors to the end shuffling

to hip-hop while the empire
disappears, tickled by the genius
that made heaven a resort
and Budweiser the King of Beers.

The Good People

History tells us they're out there
and they don't want to kill us.
History tells us they're out there
like stars buried in the galaxy,
invisible until the earth becomes
the blacker hole and they bloom
like jewels in a cave.

They don't want our passports
or sex. They don't want our rings
or our teeth. Don't mistake their
fierceness for kindness, for kind people
often do as they're told then beg
forgiveness on their knees.

The good people can't live with
forgiveness. Still, to see them
requires desperate eyes; the footsteps
of murderers approaching, God holding
your breath beneath a trash pile
or floorboards, your only hope
a distant star answering the door.

Counting the Dead

The wounded belong to somebody else.
I don't know their names or their odds.
By the time they're on my list both
clouds and doctors have moved on,
the beds and days all wear new faces.
Every army needs an army of men
good with numbers; some to count boots
and guns, others to count trucks, tanks,
prayers and sins, all to keep track of
what God has rationed.
It's dangerous work, even miles from
the front. The ground is hungry and
always shifting. Mistakes are inevitable.
Attrition is the devil. Hell is being short
Strykers or artificial limbs.
My list is where everything is
reconciled, where every guess and
every risk hits the bottom line.
The information, of course, is confidential,
until the doorbell breaks your heart.

A School Bus Ambushed by Terrorists

Somehow they rise up and fly.
Somehow they shake off the mud,
The sewage and rot and pull themselves
up to a passing wind. If you live close to
the weather you've seen them yourself
a hundred times. You know their names,
you know that wind. The children of God,
if he'll have them.

Friendly Fire

A good soldier knows to clean his gun,
knows to keep his boots combat-ready.
I was a good soldier; I feared any sound
not my breathing. I feared the coward in
my prayers and the hero in every man.
Most nights, the enemy was boredom.
We smoked and joked and jerked ourselves
to sleep. We knew our planes were shitting
hell on some other mothers' sons.
We hoped it would all be over before
new orders hit, hoped we could drive
through the rubble without inhaling.

Our prayers weren't getting through.
By 1600 we were already moving north,
tanks and jeeps snaking through sand,
ready to mop up the mess.
Their town in shambles, the hard cores
refused to leave, insisting we kill them
one by one, face to face.
We wouldn't disappoint them.
We carved each town in quarters,
erasing anything that wouldn't surrender.
The rulebook says identify the enemy
before you shoot, and that's what you'd say
if you were safe at home, asleep
on a bookshelf.

I'll let others speak for themselves
but I was frightened so my finger was
a feather on the trigger. I shot at every
shadow before it could shoot at me.

What or if I killed, I couldn't always say,
because it was dark and I let myself
be blind. The blindness made me high.

With the area secured and rumor
of the whole damn thing being over in days,
I lay impaled on my cot and slept deep in myself—
too deep to feel the air twist and spit.
Far off, a stadium crowd screamed at the crack
of a bat. What bat? I pried one eye open.
Half naked, soldiers were racing through the tent
pulling on their boots. *The sons of bitches
are bombing us!* DuRuppo yelled.
Who? I screamed back, now running myself,
juggling rifle and pants. We sprinted into
the darkness, threw ourselves down like slabs
of meat on the hot sand. Thunder exploded
in my chest as each bomb hit, the ground
punching at my face and groin. I knew
I would die if I stayed where I was.

I began crawling as fast as I could, swimming
through the sand waves crashing overhead.
Like an insect desperate for a hole on a pane
of glass, I pawed my way toward the only trench
I knew, a freshly dug latrine. Sliding in head first,
lathered in waste, I smiled to be so lucky.
But I wasn't alone in that ditch.
Two others had the same idea but too late
for any luck. The Puerto Rican kid, Estero,
was already dead. And J.J., eyes open
and still breathing, had caught something
in the head. *Our own fucking planes*, he said,
his neck wrapped in a scarf of blood.

I tried to prop him up but when I did
we both screamed, his right arm hanging
from his sleeve. I choked back the vomit.
Blood was dripping from his mouth.
You're gonna be alright, I whispered,
but he knew I was talking to myself.
His lips barely moved. *Kill me,* he said.

The bombs seemed more in the distance now
though I couldn't trust my ears to tell the truth.
A sponge of piss and blood, everything I was
reeked through and through. J.J. groaned,
his black face a ghost of grey. *Kill me, motherfucker.*
Instead, I put the barrel of the gun under
my own chin but heard his voice damn me forever.
Knowing God had damned us both I let it fall
on J.J.'s chest, I closed my eyes and pulled the trigger.

Peter Serchuk's poems have appeared in a variety of journals big and small including *Atlanta Review, Boulevard, Denver Quarterly, New Plains Review, North American Review, POEM, Poetry, South Carolina Review, Valparaiso Poetry Review* and others. Additionally, a number of his poems have been anthologized. He is the author of two poetry collections: *Waiting for Poppa at the Smithtown Diner* (University of Illinois Press) and now, *All That Remains* (WordTech Editions). He lives in Los Angeles.

CPSIA information can be obtained at www.ICGtesting.com
Printed in the USA
LVOW040249120612

285616LV00001BA/91/P